Praise for *Wound Is the O*

"Staggering. . . . [T]he beauty and brav her gentle urgency and profound decla ing, resonate in the insistent hopefulness on which her poems ultimately land." —Shannon Nakai, *Heavy Feather Review*

"Astonishingly beautiful. . . . [I]lluminated by an original light like no other." —Martina Evans, *Irish Times*

"Popa is both inheritor and innovator of the American lyric tradition. . . . This is the kind of poetry that unlocks windows of possibility within a reader." —Ellora Sutton, *Mslexia*

"Subtle and gorgeous. . . . The ecstatic language of these meditations and confessions is animated as much by pain as by joy." —*Publishers Weekly*, starred review

"A remarkable collection from an early-career poet very much making her ascendance." —*Booklist*

"Popa's elegant and moving exploration of grief and its causes and manifestations is more nuanced than simply observing that loss and living go hand-in-hand." —Sarah Kain Gutowski, *New York Journal of Books*

"This book is an astonishment. . . . *Wound Is the Origin of Wonder* reflects to us our own historical moment with unusual clarity, even as its lyric exploration of psychic and social landscapes stands outside of time." —Meghan O'Rourke

"*Wound Is the Origin of Wonder* is stunning for how it miraculously balances tenderness and terror." —Hanif Abdurraqib

"When I reached the end of this book, I wasn't ready for its spell to be broken, not yet, so I began it again." —Maggie Smith

"*Wound Is the Origin of Wonder* is a complex, searching collection, one I will be returning to for years." —Kaveh Akbar

ALSO BY MAYA C. POPA

American Faith

WOUND

IS THE ORIGIN

OF WONDER

poems

Maya C. Popa

W. W. NORTON & COMPANY
Independent Publishers Since 1923

For information about permission to reproduce selections from this book, write to
Permissions, W. W. Norton & Company, Inc., 500 Fifth Avenue, New York, NY 10110

For information about special discounts for bulk purchases, please contact
W. W. Norton Special Sales at specialsales@wwnorton.com or 800-233-4830

Manufacturing by Versa Press
Book design by Beth Steidle
Production manager: Louise Mattarelliano

Library of Congress Cataloging-in-Publication Data
Names: Popa, Maya C., 1989– author.
Title: Wound is the origin of wonder : poems / Maya C. Popa.
Description: First Edition. | New York, NY : W. W. Norton & Company, [2023]
Identifiers: LCCN 2022027176 | ISBN 9781324021360 (cloth) | ISBN 9781324021377 (epub)
Subjects: LCGFT: Poetry.
Classification: LCC PS3616.O6484 W68 2023 | DDC 811/.6—dc23
LC record available at https://lccn.loc.gov/2022027176

ISBN 978-1-324-07621-6 pbk.

W. W. Norton & Company, Inc., 500 Fifth Avenue, New York, N.Y. 10110
www.wwnorton.com

W. W. Norton & Company Ltd., 15 Carlisle Street, London W1D 3BS

1 2 3 4 5 6 7 8 9 0

We talked with each other about each other
Though neither of us spoke.

—EMILY DICKINSON

If I defer the grief, I will diminish the gift.

—EAVAN BOLAND

CONTENTS

Wonder, from the Old English wundor, *is thought to be a cognate with the German* wunde *or wound.*

DEAR LIFE

I can't undo all I have done to myself,
what I have let an appetite for love do to me.

I have wanted all the world, its beauties
and its injuries; some days,
I think that is punishment enough.

Often, I received more than I'd asked,

which is how this works—you fish in open water
ready to be wounded on what you reel in.

Throwing it back was a nightmare.
Throwing it back and seeing my own face

as it disappeared into the dark water.

Catching my tongue suddenly on metal,
spitting the hook into my open palm.

Dear life: I feel that hook today most keenly.

Would you loosen the line—you'll listen

if I ask you,

if you are the sort of life I think you are.

I

THE BENDS

When the doctor sliced open the body,
soft still to the touch, apprenticed
to expression, when the flesh

was pulled back between index and thumb
revealing the armor of breastbone,
imagine him who saw the heart froth,

the heart bubble over like soda water.
Then think of grief leaving the body,
flitting like salt to the nearby sink,

and joy like atoms joining in air
towards another living promise.
Under the night of millions of gallons

of water, the man had been building
the Brooklyn Bridge, rinsing off
the day's labors in streams warm

and patient, rainlike now. *The bends*
after the posture assumed by the afflicted
as nitrogen crept up the spine's steps.

There are still things that cannot be imagined.
The indifferent light on the surface of
the water. The wounding breath of air.

EVERYONE IS HAVING AN ISLAND VACATION

Somewhere in Greece by the white of it,
blues so soaked they emit their own light.
Admiring coastlines from lookouts on cliffs,
looking blasé in ancient temples.
I remember those summers on my father's shoulders
when the man would point to the cross
on the mountain, ask if it was raining.
Full days settled by wildflower and stone.
Green, in a word; we gave each day the full human,
and it gave us tranquil deaths: the beetle's
gem-like shell, vacant bee in the window
of an ancient tram. I was unsure anyone lived
the way I did, slowly, presently, in color.
Was often by myself speaking to a weed
pulled from the local imagination. For what
would you forfeit the real, no one asked,
before handing me the photographs.
There I am, I concede, in a red bandana
placed gently in my father's youth,
a hush of blue foothills. So this is what it was like,
or not unlike, to be me, a virgin in my father's country,
at six, in the unfinished interior. But how
to insist on other senses, all their patient sanities?
Half my body warm, the other, damp in clover.
The dirt pulled as it dried on my knees.
I was hungry, simply, and feared the mountain.
There was time to be afraid and to outlive,
unaccounted seconds in their coats of chance.
Now everyone is lined in spasms of *hereness*,

at the gym, then exiting the movie theater.
What's happened in between, mislaid inside them,
bookended by moments that endure in others.
Every feeling, cousin to some vanished one,
echoes through the halls of our aloneness.

LONGING EXPLAINED BY WILLIAM JAMES

I know the color blue when I see it, and the
flavour of a pear when I taste it;
but about the inner nature of these facts,
I can say nothing at all.

—WILLIAM JAMES

Pears will come to you if you are patient

Blue will come   a mood of green

so confusion rules all things

The mind   an appetite grammarian

summons gods from glances

full of chance antiquities

I met you in a place   that is that place

because I met you   the spine of English

softening between us

                              a village

where each   through his sewing

and weaving   utters the mimic's prayer

to memory

It is permanently summer there

                        hedgerows mostly

                a sort of slow vanishing

your image from every vantage

absented

So tugs possession   impatient and abstract

whose troubled grace   is lack.

MARGRAVINE

In the cemetery, the only available light
is shed by those wandering through,
tired, hungry, and a little put off
to be stepping on the mouths of so many
once-people. We overlook the names
ambling towards one end which is a river,
which is always, somehow, a river.
I joke you brought me here to show me
your plot, or to slay me in summer's
unabridged grass, though the joke's
that your hands will never be on me.
No future between us; we might as well be dead,
quoting Hardy to explain the little path
you sometimes take, like in a film you switch off
because life's short. Come midnight,
youths commit all sorts of crimes to prove
they're not afraid of what's coming for them.
They have the right idea, the wrong one,
or none. Either way, the grave. The flowers
growing furiously in their June bodies.
I lie about cemeteries all the time.
It's most alive at the heart of the thing
where the brush of your fingertips
against my wrist could send me begging.
Hurry, while we aren't dried up rivers.
While your mouth's not underfoot
in a permanent scream. It's most alive
at the heart of the thing, the only light,
a bright sheen given off by everything.

PRAYER

What runs through me could hardly be called piety.
It's not patience either, at least not by that name.
The pasture's dissolution into darkness,
the cow gnawing obediently without notion of infinity
and stars—God, you know all about them.

Those evenings I was sure I'd die,
you were teaching me to live; I see that now.
And the gravity of all you did not say
but left me like a map for the intuiting.
Slowly, I saw the world for what it was,

or was it I who grew familiar, that long
habit of me? These were the pains
I was granted in this life: my face in cold weather,
a throbbing at the temples. And because
these occasionally left me, all secondary anguish,

I modeled on Yours: I swam in perpetual
end of spring knowing no summer could come of it,
used the same shears to trim a leaf of poison
and its remedy; I knew enough to know what I was doing.
So often I thought that I was clever, God,

and could see the spirit moving within me
like a school of fish darting under ice.
In the lit-up scan of my left breast,
bright dashes of calcium the beautiful doctor
used her needle to guide out of me.

A metal marker forever near my heart,
my mother's heart, her mother's; we are alive,
and now, and still. I'll tell you something
I've never told a God: I've been ready for a fight,
been ready for suffering. All my allowances

came and spent and all the coffers magically
replenished. Why galaxies, God? The fit
of one palm inside another? This ache
of once—*I know, I know.* Not piety:
let me earn what I've got already.

DISQUIET: A TAXONOMY

I want to love someone I worry
is me, though it's just as often you
I worry I love when I mistake
the spoken for the intuited,
the ice for the fish beneath.

How the Buddhist described
desire's oculus, how the artist
picked a flower from a vase
and used it to paint flowers
fills me with worry. The difference

between irony and allegory,
telling mountain from molehill
or landmine. I worry I'll only
have words with which
to tell the story of what mostly

occurred outside language,
like a doctor treating for
the wrong ailment, which
doctors often do, much to
my worry. See, it's like a sun

where your voice lives in memory,
like moonlight on water—
the mixed simile worries.
Most people are dreaming
of someone else, it's what keeps
the jukebox playing all night.

I'm worried Willie Nelson was right.

ON THE SUBJECT OF BUTTERFLIES

Trying to write about them is hopeless,
those machinations colluding with air
Turgenev compared to withered maple.

Sentimental, resigned to knowing better,
and wondering still at the paperwork
of flight, armed with nets to breed

a tortured familiarity. Do they recognize
the desperation of our doing,
believing desire should end in evidence,

or after a life at ease with transformation,
are they so sure to be returned
to that first moment when anything

might still become of them
in fate's commanding and indifferent hand?

IN THE MUSEUM OF CHILDHOOD

It's yours I remember,
and Larkin's, who called his
a forgotten boredom.

How it might just as well
have never happened,
though it did once,

it happened once, to you,
in a house with a moat
and no heating,

twin voices boiling over
in the kitchen below.
You'd survive it all,

which is to say, forsake,
those days turning in you
like a pinwheel still,

that base from which
language understands
its failure. There was time

to be apart and still a part
of something human
before the usual forfeiture

of green to cities, days blunted
by the millstone of duty.
Now the hours blink back

with the eyes of roadside
animals, and the disks shrink
with not enough of anything

worth keeping. You could weep
for all you did not know then
was a blessing, the voices

hurt and angry but living
nonetheless, the highway throbbing
with its dreamed-of passages.

The museum makes converts
out of visitors. I lug youth's
icons inside me and believe

we bear that loss we caused
by our arriving. We were never
loved by anything

the way tomorrow loved us then.

GENII LOCI

All along, the world had referred to a real place
where it was hard to leave the car if parked too near a hedge.

To race the body towards pleasure in the backseat
held no appeal, though the image had its salvageable moments,
the hand that gripped the wheel gentling the flesh,
hitch of breath at an unexpected angle.

Not for us, we said, chastened by memory's make-believe.

Besides, the humiliating inelegance,
the onlookers with rucksacks that double as sleeping bags,
the ones with binoculars come expressly for the doggers,
watching couples strip down to what's left at the beginning.

No appetite so large it could not be filled
behind closed doors, we agreed, a joke we'd return to politely.

About the animal of the body, I have learned
it's in no hurry to be sated or stilled.
It lives to serve the error that confounds it,
to wrestle with buttons in the mind's backseat.

No imagination safe enough from love
which swears by a map that leads nowhere.

We could drive ourselves and each other out with it,
could wave goodbye or wait—we could never stop waiting.

AFTER

Skymiles of starlings over the penitentiary.

December a descant and a North Star
like a North Star.

Twice a day, the sun.

The hand of wind over the mountains.

The rest will become, disappear by becoming.

Dark of plenty, of fracture. God's dark
of perfect recall.

What earth is this if not ripe for threshing?

What joy it was, and how we knew what joy it was.

WOUND IS THE ORIGIN OF WONDER

The bee that worshiped the mouths of those flowers
dropped to your window like a spent priest,
its thud comedic in the coded silence.
You were making a change to the order of your hours,
had announced as much in the prior moment,
and if I thought of Virgil's *Georgics,* it was only
not to mention them. I brought my eye
to its abdomen, offered an ounce of my human life.
What would you do with the knowledge
that I'd grieve for a bee? Someone like me
could be played by the threat of endings.
I'll lose you one day, have lost you always,
a long ongoing Westwardness of thought.
It's not metaphor that bees make honey
of themselves while language only dreams
the hunted thing. Let's be hungry a little
while longer. Let's not hurt each other if we can.

THE TEARS OF THINGS

In a restaurant with mandolins affixed
to the ceiling, which you remembered
visiting at intervals of childhood,
the drive from Stroud into London's
bright heaving with a hunger more
than an aptitude for hope,

we spoke of school days, ink stone
dark as grackle, lines for baths
in winter's thinning light, then fumbled
towards the past that's part invention,
the town whose mills were powered
by rivers, fields that froze like strangers

hearing their names called. Weddings
took their cue from funerals, the locals
bouncing home from hedge to hedge,
though not without its charms, you said,
the grouse stone-heavy come July.
A life forged out of spent alternatives,

enchanting as a liquor brewed by moonlight.
All night, I listened for my cause
in words blue-shifted under longing's reach
until slow aerated rain began at last,
and we set out in the shadow of an
unnamed thing. We saw, in an absent-

minded wish, a loose stitch, the mind

in the velvet of the matter. No—
it was the sort of seeing that unfastens
the *lacrimae rerum*, tears of things.
We drowned, not knowing we stood in water.

II

FIFE

The white sun has her way here,
raising a fog like an atomized star
over ruins
and the heron standing on one leg.

Listen: everything is listening
to the North Sea retreating
like a voice before sleep.

Out there, the beloved
is slipping through time; otherwise,
you might see without inquiry.

When will the fog lift,
by what doing?

A faint hiss like a stone's lament.

A faint hiss—that is
your own life now, hurrying
from one light into another.

YEAR

I wouldn't be who I am
if I could bear the foliage,

the hour losing
its precious light

like a knight bleeding out
through a hole in the armor.

I wouldn't be, if I could,
any more than that—

light on burnt leaves
while the hurt worked

its anchor, the chain eased
slowly like a tongue,

a word for grief that
doesn't rhyme with *thief.*

Any day now, autumn.
Winter any day.

I've shot my arrow
and lived by its arc

and still, the hours
won't acquit.

The first time we met
we said goodbye,

then we never stopped
saying it.

THE OWL

Took off from the field again
      away from you and back in my direction.

We share an owl now—we did not mean
      for this to happen. It hovers

between us, a symbol and debt, sleeps
      in a country neither recognizes

until we're face to face—then, it's familiar,
      and it's impossible not to laugh.

Of course, there's an owl. You're the owl
      in the belfry set off by noon bells.

I'm the owl circling the wounded land.
      Among the difficulties of caring

for something metaphorical
      is the guarantee it will one day

become something else, and it's hard to say
      for certain when the transformation's final.

How you woke one morning at a job
      you hated, in a mind you'd wrestled

into gentleness, and nothing made sense
      except the way I listened.

You burned for me; the owl was a candle
     by whose flame I could see

my own value clearly: the second chance,
     the double life tiptoed watchfully around.

The feeling only a wild bird knows
     whose head turns 270 degrees,

is silent in flight and blends
     with its settings, whose talons can

withstand any sort of landing. That,
     a neckless wonder, strips

ligament from flesh. Something so polite
     about enduring its violence

and hoping only to remain in favor,
     watch the bones assemble

in the shape of a vole. There are ways
     to fail an owl, for metaphor

to fail. I remember you—the dusk
     we wrought by listening.

The long hunt we made of night.

LETTERS IN WINTER

There is not one leaf left on that tree
on which a bird sits this Christmas morning,

the sky heavy with snow that never arrives,
the sun itself barely rising. In the overcast

nothingness, it's easy to feel afraid,
overlooked by something that was meant

to endure. It's difficult today to think
clearly through pain, some actual,

most imagined; future pain I try lamely
to prepare myself for by turning your voice

over in my mind, or imagining the day
I'll no longer hug my father, his grip

tentative but desperate all the same.
At the café, a woman describes lilacs

in her garden. She is speaking of spring,
the life after this one. The first thing

to go when I shut the book between us
is the book; silence, its own alphabet,

and still something so dear about it.
It will be spring, I say over and over.

I'll ask that what I lost not grow back.
I see how winter is forbidding:

it grows the heart by lessening everything else
and demands that we keep trying.

I am trying. But oh, to understand us,
any one of us, and not to grieve?

READING

The medium says it is a past-life connection;
two lives, she amends, at least two.

This, my life to mourn you,
to work through that other life

in which you died, a soldier, writing letters
from a border, and I never found a way

back into daylight. Needless to say,
this was not the good news I had hoped for.

I thought she'd offer something
conventionally hopeful, direct me

to a trap door I failed to see.
There was victory in the form

of wands or swords, I couldn't say which.
An end to grief so utter, I'm the mouth

it speaks with. What do I do?
Thread the past through the present's eye?

Ask that we meet in the blasted heath between?
She said, no, no, that won't be necessary.

Just forgive him: first for living, then for dying.
What are days for if not to let go of days.

AT *CUTTY SARK*

1.

The clipper without
sail or shroud,

a shell through which
the city gleamed

silver-blue at midweek
dusk. It was easy

to picture us returning here
in spring, strolling

the Naval College's
orderly greens,

once site of Bella Court
built by the Duke

of Gloucester, at some
other time a hospital.

Between chestnuts
and desultory statues,

on the south bank
where the water

laps up steel,
we would have relished

the past's peculiar
compulsions,

the ceiling painted
for the naval pensioners—

there was a world
before this one:

it moved like sun
over skin.

2.

At dinner, I showed you
pictures of New York,

*like the Wilcoxes, the objects
just so at Howard's End.*

I'll say I didn't know it then,
not that I didn't heed—

anything can be afforded
in the beginning.

You were a principle
of forfeiture;

I see that now, a hope
made void by prior hope.

A skeleton ship
and London lit up

through it, the horizon
at capacity already,

suffused with an easy
absence of you,

stretched pale and
indifferent and new.

THE PEACOCKS

in Holland Park don't care who loves them.
They are like stones at the bottom of cool rivers
and it's only our wandering that brings them
into focus, its own kind of foreboding.
It's not only color and scale that endears them.
It's the way they cannot be conceived of fully
without blinking back a dread at splendor
so near a public waste bin, the likelihood of failure.
The staccato of orange against blue—really,
how much more will this world enrage us
with its beauty, even as it leans towards last
assessments. And haven't I minded you like this,
a cartographer patiently charting planets
before going mad with light? Haven't I taken
that footpath down a woodland labeled *dark*;
do not enter; *idle*; *want*? Oh, but for the ode of it.
The life that can't be lived behind the eyelids.
And you, a fruit there somewhere in the branches.
A bird that will not scare or fly.

DREAM VISION

A long tradition of hallucinations,
    flocks in patterns that silence
        the augur.

The dream tents in *Gilgamesh* Enkidu built
    en route to Cedar Forest
        so the signs would find them.

It was visions of passion I most feared,
    your hands at my waist, my chin
        at your shoulder—

your breath just once and I'd have been done for,
    awake enough to know how grim
        a dream could be.

Would have mislaid North—I'd have been
    like Gilgamesh above
        the slaughtered flesh

of the Bull of Heaven, dreaming his love
    with a herd at night before sending
        the body down the river.

For each day you have not written, a large ship
    has floated up the driveway; no one
        has boarded or come off.

THE PRESENT SPEAKS OF PAST PAIN

It's that hour of dusk
when the sky is awash
in waning light, when, if we might

forgive each other, this would be
the hour for it.

I lay down beneath a yellow tree.

I understood I could hold on to the past
or be happy.

Then, nothing. You did not appear to me.

The sky filled with stars
that had been there already.

THE SCORES

The stones are alive here, clotted with mollusks,
bearded and slick with sea grass.

All night, I watched the blue adjust,
slow exhale at light's command.

The shoreline and its principle of hunger
foregone that something else might overtake.

It isn't like the love we know that brings us flowers.

It's the love whose imminence
is certain blinding, the split shell that draws blood.

Of course, the tragedy would be to want
nothing with want, to gaze at the North Sea

and see only a futility. How then to look
so that the light's hand might move you

like water, returning to the same conclusion,
hauling its mind back to the harbor,

tolling a bell that won't let.

AFTER A VASE BROKEN BY MARCEL PROUST

What we know, we come to know
by its undoing; there is no permanent

exhibit here. Like August stars, we offer
temporary light, our lives measured

in latitudes of loss, the longest distance
between any two points in time.

And, errant, we are covetous: the humble
vase broken by Marcel Proust re-glued,

imbued with preciousness. He believed
that grief develops the mind. What is

the mind if not that surface upon which
the world can be endlessly rebroken?

You hold me in yours as you walk to the sea
and my clothes catch on brier and bramble.

The view familiar, like a page from a book
we once wrote, its single copy, in a library that burned.

M40

The wind moves the leaves
in multiple directions
like a mind caught between alternatives.

Bright arrows of sunlight
between lashes, the branches
cleared revealing nests.

One day, this grief
will seal from feeling,
a cool politeness round a thin raised scar.

The crows are hard at work again,
driving their beaks
into frozen fields.

What does it matter, you think.
Matter! Matter! they reply.

WOUND IS THE ORIGIN OF WONDER

A cross-breeze between this life
and the imagined one.

I am stuck in an *almost* life,
in an almost time. If I could say,

but I cannot, and so on. Sunlight
dizzies through the barren trees,

the skyline, a blue fog against
a yellow light, and on the highway

every Westward car blinds me.
Every surface reflects

that quiet understanding: decisions
have been made, irreversible decisions

to upend beauty for something
approximate—the airport hotel,

its Eiffel Tower on the roof,
a playground near the public storage.

Beyond, bridges like monuments
to fracture, and a sign for Pain Law:

not metaphor, but litigation.
Who would not, given acreage

in another's mind, lie there
for a while to watch the sky be sky.

LETTER TO NOAH'S WIFE

You are never mentioned on Ararat
or elsewhere, but I know a woman's hand
in salvation when I see it. Lately,
I'm torn between despair and ignorance.
I'm not a vegetarian, shop plastic,
use an air conditioner. Is this what happens
before it all goes fluvial? Do the selfish
grow self-conscious by the withering
begonias? Lately, I worry every black dress
will have to be worn to a funeral.
New York a bouillon, eroded filigree.
Anything but illness, I beg the plagues,
but shiny crows or nuclear rain.
Not a drop in London May through June.
I bask in the wilt by golden hour light.
Lately, only lately, it is late, tucking
our families into the safeties of the past.
My children, will they exist by the time
it's irreversible? Will they live
astonished at the thought of ice
not pulled from the mouth of a machine?
Which parent will be the one to break
the myth: the Arctic wasn't Sisyphus's
snowy hill. Noah's wife, I am wringing
my hands not knowing how to know
and move forward. Was it you
who gathered flowers once the earth
had dried? How did you explain the light
to all the animals?

LATE GENESIS

Now the earth was full of violence, jaywalkers,
sports deities, faces on skin and screens
worshiped evenly.

With everything visible, it was hard
to see the world,

to believe you were another meat.

There was malice, but mostly
a kind of grief.

Leaves on trees but a shiver in the daylight.

Chiefly, it was language
that confounded them—

permafrost suggesting permanence,

not the flux of a fjord,
not the forfeiture.

The people combed for answers
without footprint, ones hedonists
would recognize as relevant,

(these were hung like sneakers from a power line),

but the picture of a polar bear
perched atop an icecap
made everyone feel lonely and unclean.

They wondered such a thing had ever existed,
a knoll of living snow, eyes plucked
from a child's coat.

                    Hadn't it all
seemed beholden to them?

Newfoundland to Vancouver,
McClure to Bering Strait.

Noah was 500 when the floods came,
his children—Shem, Ham, Japheth—grown.

All the sons had sons after the flood,
as ice takes its cue from ice

before it ends, in elegant agreement.

MILTON VISITS GALILEO IN FLORENCE

Hard to say if what they saw
was geometry or God, galaxies roiling
wordlessly each night, a summary of light
painted fresh across the firmament.

Ink bringing daybreak into Eden, the angels,
listless in their graces, latent good
pooling with nothing to war over.

A jug of water on the table between them
like an artifact of loneliness, the telescope's
moons on Satan's shield—it was, after all,
a human friendship, full of mortality's tokens.

Both went blind in their old age.

Begin again in darkness, life says sometimes.
Picture the trees burning in autumn,
the earth's relief, at last, at being fallen.

GHOST CRABS

are mostly speculations on shape,
a way to say *ghost* with scientific
aplomb. They haunt a stretch
of Atlantic from Nantucket to Brazil,
their numbers dwindling like everything
that isn't us.
                         Jeeps driving
down the beach pack the sand too firmly,
entombing the crabs in their burrows
overnight. I don't know that the world
was ever more forgiving, the lorries
less heavy with stolen bodies,
the drownings fewer over holiday weekends.

The ghost crabs come like spies
and it is beautiful to hope for them,
over the bright channels of the sea
and our unbright moorings.

                    You will know
when it is time to mourn, they seem to say.
Today, I glimpse their rushed transparencies
and think, it could never be too early.

A HUMBLING

Here it hangs like a teardrop in resin
the moment I might have fractured my life,
shredded it like a paper and started afresh

with the memory of paper nevertheless,
this tear in the cloth un-yet and unleavened.
Or sweeter; might have bent it, drawn it

like a bow aimed at the body's faithless
alternate. The moment plays on
repeating its inactions, asking faint stars

for directions in the night. Moves
the rain like a calculated wish, and you,
a phantom fishbone in the throat,

the fish, the most beautiful fish;
the sea, the most beautiful sea.

REPRISE

Oh, but I could mourn you all day long,
the sky, a spool of undyed wool
only you'd know what to make of.

You once believed the moon pitch black,
a flashlight pointed at refracting coal.

You were a child, and I will never
have a child with you, that wasted
tenderness where might have lived a world.

On earth, it will matter little that we met,
our days like rivers at the mouth
of a sea so cold, so quiet, so blue.

DURESS

An old habit by now this new life bleaching lemons,
        careful to remove, first gloves, then mask,
                careful not to rush the work

of being careful. For this, we live
        a little injured through our hours. We live—
                what greater mercy is admissible?

By day, the branches with fist-sized magnolias,
        by night, the last of winter's winds,
                so you might believe the sirens

were a single siren. Often, I've wanted,
        not death, but disappearance,
                evaporation, a bloodless

self-banishment. But the times call for patience,
        not terror or time travel, not Eros
                or negative capability.

I remember it was joy once that stopped breath,
        complicated joy—it wasn't easy
                as all that. I thought of you,

the hangman's knot we'd made of language,
        thought I'd say, once and for all,
                thought I'd say it all, only,

we weren't dying. We were alive—the point
was to outlive . . . this new life
bleaching lemons, and the voice

of attention asking what you've missed.

SIGNAL

*To exchange signals with Mars—without
fantasizing, of course—that is a task worthy
of a lyric poet.*

—OSIP MANDELSTAM

Of course, the secret aim
of losing you those months
had been to find you again.

I went looking for what
had once belonged to you,
found a voice to cauterize

the wound. I made it through
April, May, June; it seemed
I had outsmarted grief

but pulled the hanged man
card repeatedly—the self-same
sorrow said a different way.

You who cannot hear me
without injury, I whisper,
I damage the throat like this,

I, my own entrapment
and hardest to forgive.
Only this life still and all

its boxes filled, its hours
spent fretting over living wills,
the horror of numbers

and headlines on Mars—
more water, more life
where it cannot be touched.

THEY ARE BUILDING A HOSPITAL

On the field outside my home, a field
hospital, in an actual field, the great American
Oak on one end, the Tupelo on the other.
They have laid white tarp over the boggy grass
and raised a series of insulated tents.
It has blossomed overnight like a dark circus,
machines to dehumidify the air,
cots like dollhouse furniture and intricate
machines to keep alive those whose bodies
are resigned to leaving. An orchestra
of discipline and calculated faith,
of power cords and outlets maneuvered
around trees, of hoping rain holds
and spring reads the room: the human beings
are desperate. They have built a hospital
where, in other days, I walked my dog,
counting no blessing but the one I chased,
who startled strangers on blankets
before stretching on the grass. How happy
I was not knowing how happy, walking
the path along the field's perimeter,
watching the sky flare its oranges and pinks,
reflect a cool purple off the leaves.
Idling in goodness, letting the mind loose
over the life let it. I thought forever,
did not think, for so much of gladness
was thoughtlessness. Now I mourn
the hours from the safety of my health,
stand a little lost at what proceeds

the mourning. They are building a hospital—
the whir of engines stirs the animals,
a melody, a dirge the robins sing.

PESTILENCE

I.

It began with a continent on fire.

Any way you turned the globe,
the flames bent with the wrist,
the animals—*God, the animals*—in treetops, singed.

The omens were there; we'd erred,
but the charge was mostly metaphorical.

We were not the animals.

In moments like these, the mind resists knowing
with any precision how others lived,
or else, it is a tax paid disbelievingly.

The fire seen widening from outer space
and nothing to lessen the undoing.

Life was objectionable, still the mind
to greet it like a river winding into blindness.

The Chinese year of the rat and this,
its opening act.

2.

Like Lady Macbeth, I proceeded
from one bad dream to the next,

held loose the reins of life,
horse bent by a river of tears.

What a way to fall out with daylight,
blinded by the actual,

the unimaginable repeatedly imagined.
Life was contagion; everything was life.

3.

Those days it hurt to be in the world,
the only thing to be done was to pay attention.

A shock of white blossoms like antique lace
appearing in the window overnight.

Times were extraordinary,
yes, everyone could see that.

Conditions were war-like;
even the doctors were frightened.

When you factored in death by suffocation . . .
Everyone was *monitoring the situation.*

All the while, nature cheered for itself,
the dogwood lit up by its own color.

Not irony, but pardon, I reminded myself.
Not irony, but spring.

4.

On the second day of spring, the families emerged
as though the times had never threatened them.

They were showing their children, yes, here's gladness still,
and look, how legible the little book of life.

The trees have rushed their flowers; it is a season of emergency.

Some compulsions, of course, had been pre-existing;
naming, for instance: *Crab Apple, Redbud, Magnolia.*

Someone had planted purple tulips, had imagined
the future, and here it was, arterial at dusk.

New flowers, new version of familiar long hours.

One afternoon, it hailed, great frozen handfuls
on the Callery, blossoms flushed with snow.

I took two baths and spent the daylight reading,
the hours fleeing and formless. *Pleasure,*

the body insists, though the mind resists that reading.

5.

In dreams, I was ill
and woke unsure that I was well.

What did "well" even look like
those days that I had been it—

well? I had been the sort of person . . .

I had been the sort
to look forward all day to the day.

In the mirror, I lifted my shirt,
the flesh growing lax beneath.

Through the window,
watched the occasional pedestrian

now a soldier
serving this city of panic.

6.

Friends fed the day hope
like a broken fever,

articles about dolphins
in Venetian canals.

By then, the hospitals
had flowered white tents,

bodies transferred
from windows

to the makeshift
morgues below.

To picture the coolers
made the soul detach

and ask to be shipped
to a nearby planet.

I was afraid and knew
how to be afraid,

scrubbing everything that came
in contact with the body.

Some joked there'd be
a generation born from this.

Who could treat the body
as anything but risk?

7.

A mouthful of black tea confirming taste.
Scent of bleach rubbed gently on the mail.

Something is meant to be improving
but something has mislaid the nights, the days.

On wet pavement, the robins reflect
whole robins made shimmering cement.

We who kept man and nature separate,
did we expect no hidden charge,

or was it knowing our debt
that slowed belief?

Is this the carnival to which
we'd always planned on arriving?

The trees looked mostly alike all year
except on the weeks you saw their flowers.

Parachutes of pollen in the sun,
as though the earth had every

intention to hold on.

8.

In April, I walked in the middle of the street
testing an appetite for life against
an appetite for peace.

I searched all eyes for similar crisis;
come evening, clapped for what had spared us,
a pantomime of happiness engineered under duress.

It was death that wanted us alive.

9.

When the sirens slowed, I was too numb
to be relieved.

When others were relieved, I was too othered
to be anything but what had happened.

Tents flapping in strong winds,
patients under rain pelting the marquee
paralyzed atop last summer's grass.

It will take longer to shed this panic
than the trees their memories of sleep

or winter's interrogation, snapping back
each branch, asking *you, will you endure this strife*?

It happened to us all, this life.

10.

Each day I remember
Each day I strategically forgot
Each day I can still taste smell long
can swallow whole lungfulls
of air unaided   hurt in all the places
owned by memory   hour after hour
in these the lessons
the days have slowly leaked
the heart broken on the same fault
differently each time   how human

is the future   will it let us let
I am listening through my terror for yours
that I might hold it between us
in the thunderclap of summer
. . .

what is that   who is that now   clapping

ALL THAT IS MADE

The trees were on the verge of rebirth so sudden
you'd miss it from one day to the next,

would be suddenly alive in it, the pale green bending open
to reveal what we'd always suspected was the case:

that every bright thing has at its heart a hiddenness
it offers when you've just about stopped looking.

In her thirtieth year, Julian was dying. No other way
to describe the proceeding of events, the widening gap

between two kinds of life: the one lived and the one
remembered. And Christ came to where she lay

fevered and helpless, sat by her bedside in velvet robes,
and opened his palm to show her a hazelnut

saying *this is all that is made.* I wouldn't know mercy
unless it looked like this, and I'd mistake it for love,

though that, too, is what it is. I understand
if you're not prepared to believe in miracles,

the hours passed from one invisible hand to the next,
but Julian lived to seventy-three in the fourteenth century.

Maybe life's little more than our own blindness easing;
look, he said, *keep looking.* How small and round our suffering.

IN EDEN

There were reasons not to eat.
For one, a snake that spoke in meter,
and the light falling just so
on the fruit of Baroque still-life.

On earth, it's sleep that interrupts
the feeding. Still, your hands
will find me in a dream,
and I'll bring them to my lips

though they're nothing like the quince.
I'd like to be less hungry,
placid like a saint, with nothing
but polite appreciation for the world.

Maybe then I'd find the living
reasonable to part with,
the blue moons and red ones
seasonally beheld—and people—

their expression like ripples
on water. I'd row out to that
horizon where nothing needs,
at last at ease with the order of things.

In Eden, everything answered
when you called it, the snake
already knowing all our names.

AQUARIUM

Imagine this: your favorite display
at the aquarium, brackish, backlit by strips
of black light, part marvel, part feat
of hydroengineering. In the cavernous
hall of that oceanic theater, everything
is dark except for this—and, yes, there are fish,
sandwiched between anemones
which fail to sting them, the placard explains.

That's what the surface of the mind is like, I said
when you could smell the air-conditioned carpet,
stone roses, neon pebbles like El Greco
frescoes, and the glass is smudged
where fingers failed to reach, and failing,
caused a momentary fog. The mind is admired,
is haunted by other minds; we call this
any number of things, love or reading . . .

What are we doing? I never asked you,
there are bleachings of all sorts from the above.
We know that beauty distracts from poison—
is that why we're standing here with gloves?
The fish swim in circles that approximate falling.
Outside, the crows are digging at the grass.
The season is turning, turning, turning.

EVERGREEN

You send me a picture in a knitted hat
in what looks to be a Christmas tree dispensary.
I think to reply with a story about Coleridge
who sometimes shared a memory about his son
in front of an engraving of a storm at sea,
and the little boy asking, *Where's the ship?*

You're holding a pine you will cover in trifles
and try to keep the cats from urinating on,
the children ecstatic that way adults seldom manage,
contented until a headache redirects from recipes
to WebMD. The come-to-Jesus about Santa Claus
has happened already; they'll want to hear

how you met your wife, whose boombox
was outside whose window all night. This life,
its crunch of cereal underfoot, is the only one
you know to listen for, the sleep of a shepherd
spent on its flock. To your right in the picture
is a boy with eyes your color and her shape.

How darling, I say, through bandages of grief;
what's never given cannot properly be taken
away. Like the ship that could not call for help
because it wasn't painted in the first place.
My own children are refractive as soap bubbles.
Some days, I see the dark bramble of their hair,

others, nothing, a heartbreak far from happening.
But it's possible to mourn them along
with your hands which, moving steadily against
a cutting board, have freed a line of ginger men
from slabs of dough. There are ways to give the mind
the illusion of movement; snow, for instance,

so faint it seems at first like nothing. Then,
it's like the seconds before fainting: pinpricks
of traffic, and you'd better sit down.
The tree grays and wilts around its ornaments,
its string of lights with one bulb perennially
missing. There's also chasing within yourself

a kind of peace. The day is full of defeats,
so you get to practice that. How the white
looks lovely now, but later comes and soon.

NOT THE WOUND, BUT WHAT THE WOUND IMPLIES

Who can say
what the tulips dream
in a hard frost,

the sky as cold
as it is clear
and still unreadable.

Or how pain
decides what stays
in memory, a gift

broken by the time
it reaches us,
silvered, gleaming with age.

ALL INNER LIFE RUNS AT SOME DELAY

like the martyr amazed at hunger's
slow subsiding.

The rain at last arrived and with it
the peculiar compulsion to keep living.

On suffering, philosophers
were always undecided:

to school an intelligence and make it
a soul, the wound is where
the light enters us, and so on.

The wound is where the light enters us.

There shines the face of the beloved
like a headlamp in the dark.

LES NEIGES D'ANTAN

In Lyon, the lovers of the past
are picking up handfuls
of powdered snow.

I watch them in the video
a friend sends colored
in confectionary pastels.

They are safe from the fear
of the world boiling over,
sons lost along the German border.

Villon asked about the snows
of yesteryear sensing there'd been
a diminishment perhaps.

It wasn't that long ago
we walked in autumn,
the silence between us

its own snow, our longing
the language of manuscripts
illuminated painstakingly by hand.

I didn't bend. You didn't.
We were wintered by the thought.
But the lovers are rushing

towards where the clip fades
into immovable darkness.
It will be 1914, the fatal cough,

the Hiroshima Mosler safe.
It will be a trying age
and then another.

It's plain we didn't see
the future coming. Even spring
came and left as a surprise.

Where are you now, snow
that vanishes with touch,
snow which cannot be

sped up but sleeps
where the past falls,
is always falling.

WOUND IS THE ORIGIN OF WONDER

Fiction is the house of many windows,
        James said, and I sat at each one
                peering at a world

that trembled—or was that me instead,
        quivering in the face
                of all I made by looking,

unable to amend the plot or bend
        the hand. Like all falls, we came at ours
                by pleasure, all languages

seconded, learned by constraint—
        no way to say *look* and *away*
                and mean *un-lone me.*

Like gods, we made our kingdom hungry.
        Our appetites' agreement
                we called love,

though it was nearer the mirror
        than mercy. Sweet solstice,
                soul cousin, *Vita Nuova*'s

Beatrice—do you hear our onceness
        beating at the door? How the past
                outlasts on either end,

though we'd like to burn out in oracular
    blindness. What doom
        to be beheld: you sing

when you should tremble. Will you leave me
    my wondering; will it be as when
        snow falls heavy on trees,

and thou art felled?

THERE MUST BE A MEANING

Here, there is nothing to be fought.
The way things are is in such a way
as to be intimated then forgotten.

The heat of shapes registers as color,
an occasional dark purple in the leaves,
a shining fracture in the cliff's silt.

And if you looked at an angle,
the island would vanish, the estate
of the image dissolved like salt.

It's the way with some things too sweet
to be lived out. I've buried you each day
in the dirt of a life I keep tilling,

dazzled by the sunlight that tenders it,
the rain amending her position midair,
time's unraveling towards later time.

The past is a country of held breaths
misread as silence, or the way things
had to be. But I am trying to see

what the land means instead
of what the mind means in the relaying.
Somewhere inside me is the understanding

that water isn't actually blue. What it
aspires to, then, may be what I mean.

SPRING

Time persists, yes, I can see there are new branches.

The grass, first in a line of transformations,
seemingly risen overnight.

Color is pouring back into the hours,
or forgiveness, whatever the case may be.

With one decisive tug at the earth, the robin's drawn forth
a shimmering worm,

with such precision, it is almost a cruel pleasure.

This, the nightmare we dreamed but did not wake from.

Time is passing, I concede.   A squirrel leaps
from one branch to another.

A hawk studies the field at dusk.

The park announces the season over and over
to no one,

and the silence cranes to listen.

Terraces of light now that the day is longer.

When joy comes, will I be ready, I wonder.

ACKNOWLEDGMENTS

I am grateful to the editors of the following journals in which these poems first appeared:

Academy of American Poets Poem-A-Day, *The American Poetry Review, Bath Magg, Inque, Jewish Currents, Oxford Review of Books, PN Review, Poetry Ireland, Poetry London, Poetry, The Adroit Journal, The Atlantic, The Baffler, The Guardian, The Kenyon Review, The London Magazine, The Los Angeles Review of Books, The Nation, The New Republic, The New Statesman, The Paris Review, The Poetry Review, The Scores, The Stinging Fly, The Times Literary Supplement, The Yale Review,* and *Wildness.*

"In the Museum of Childhood" was published in the 2020 Bridport Prize Anthology.

"Signal" first appeared in *The London Magazine* and was reprinted in the anthology *Poems from Pandemia* (Cork, Ireland: Southword Editions, 2020).

"*Wound* Is the Origin of Wonder" (p. 54) first appeared in *The Yale Review* and was reprinted in the anthology *World Out of Reach* (New Haven, CT: Yale University Press, 2020).

"Letter to Noah's Wife" appeared on the Academy of American Poets *Poem-A-Day* and is forthcoming in the anthology *Without a Doubt* (New York: New York Quarterly).

A portion of the manuscript received second place in the Alpine Fellowship Poetry Prize judged by John Burnside and Gillian Clarke.

Several of these poems appear collected in the chapbook *Dear Life*, Smith|Doorstop Books, 2022.

My most profound gratitude to my family, friends, and teachers. In particular, to my PhD supervisor at Goldsmiths, University of London, Maura Dooley, without whose brilliance and compassion the book would not exist; to Peter Straus at RCW Literary Agency, Jill Bialosky at W. W. Norton, Anya Backlund at Blue Flower Arts; Peter Sansom at Smith|Doorstop Books; and all of the journal editors who gave these poems early homes.

My love, admiration, and thanks to writer friends: Anthony Anaxagarou, Catherine Barnett, Caroline Bird, Sam Copeland, Saskia Hamilton, Lizzie Harris, Laura Kirk, Deborah Landau, Jen Levitt, Jenny Lewis, Robert Macfarlane, Jamie McKendrick, Coco Mellors, Meghan O'Rourke, Betsey Osborne, Christine Schutt, Nicole Sealey, Brenda Shaughnessy, Craig Morgan Teicher, Rupert Thomson, Brad Whitehurst, and Jenny Xie.

To Rob Burnett for his warmth and generosity, and for housing me in idyllic Vermont, where I wrote happily for months.

To John Loughery for more than is easily summarized.

To Emily Dunn and Kelly Rodigas for their daily love and support.

And to Sam and my parents—for everything.

NOTES

"Disquiet: A Taxonomy": The italicized lines loosely quote the musician and singer Willie Nelson.

"In the Museum of Childhood": Larkin calls his childhood "a forgotten boredom" in the poem "Coming."

"After": The final line is adapted from Nadezhda Mandelstam's letter to Osip Mandelstam: "What joy it was, and how we always knew what joy it was."

"The Tears of Things" refers to the Latin phrase *lacrimae rerum*, or "tears of things," from book I, line 462 of Virgil's *Aeneid*.

"Dream Vision" is for Jenny Lewis.

"After a Vase Broken by Marcel Proust" was inspired by Stephen Greenblatt's "Resonance and Wonder," which refers to an exhibit that featured a vase shattered by Marcel Proust.

"All Inner Life Runs at Some Delay": In a letter to John Reynolds (1817), Keats writes: "Do you not see how necessary a World of Pains and troubles is to school an Intelligence and make it a soul?" Versions of the phrase "The wound is where the light enters you" are attributed to the thirteenth-century mystic poet Rumi.

"Les Neiges D'Antan": "Mais où sont les neiges d'antan?" ("Where are the snows of yesteryear?") is a line from François Villon's poem "Ballade des dames du temps jadis."

"*Wound* Is the Origin of Wonder" (p. 89): Henry James's actual remark is "The house of fiction has in short not one window, but a million. . . ."